A Place Called Aullwood

in Southwestern Ohio:
Its Flowers, Woodlands and Meadows
Photographic Essay
by Allan L. Horvath
PhD, APSA

Christmas, 1996

To my photographer with
a keen eye for beauty —
your patience and creativity
come through that lens!
Love,
Alana

ISBN 0-9654152-0-1
Copyright © 1996 Allan L Horvath Publications
Printed in the United States of America
First Edition

Acknowledgements

Major Sponsors
Five Rivers MetroParks
Virginia Kettering
Roy and Pat Horvath

Anonymous Corporate Sponsor
Biebel & French
Bowser - Morner, Inc.
Children's Medical Center
City of Dayton Mayor and Commissioners
Germaine International Language Center
Good Samaritan Hospital
Carolyn Talbot Hoagland
Julie Horvath
Lockwood, Jones & Beals, Inc.
Ruth Mead
Mr. and Mrs. Harry S. Price, Jr.
Mr. and Mrs. Ralph Reahard, Jr.
Sally Reahard
United Theological Seminary

Special Assistance
Additional photos   - Ben Jakobowski, APSA
                     - Charity Krueger
                     - Duryea. Morton
Consulting editor   - Carol Mattar
Design   - Patterson Graphics
Editorial intern   - Melissa McMonigle
Printing   - The Nielsen Company
Project advisor   - Bob Siebenthaler
Research assistance - Suzan MacKenzie
                     - Montgomery County
                       Historical Society
                     - Dr. Joseph Wilson

Foreword

A Place Called Aullwood is a most superb blend of talent. In this book, photos and text combine to inspire and educate the reader. It is about a country garden, a nature center and a children's farm: the dream of a devoted couple, John and Marie Aull. Hence, the name Aullwood.

The photos come from a vast collection of nature slides by the late Allan L. Horvath, PhD, APSA, photographer and geologist. The text is by Paul E. Knoop, Jr., former director of the Aullwood Audubon Center and retired education co-ordinator for Aullwood Audubon Center and Farm.

Allan L. Horvath

I first knew Allan when he was associate professor of geology at the University of Dayton. He often stopped by my office at the Dayton-Montgomery County Park District's Leland Center headquarters to offer his services as a volunteer. Allan conducted geology and photography workshops for the Park District, the Dayton Museum of Natural History, and Aullwood.

Allan had a successful career as a photographer, his photos exhibited worldwide. He had spent several years as a geologist in the oil fields of New Mexico before coming to teach at U.D. After retiring, he returned to photography and wrote books. A technical work, How to Create Photographic Special Effects (1979), was followed by the photo-essay The Hills of Hocking (1986), both very popular books. Allan became friends with Marie Aull and was a familiar visitor to Aullwood during the late 1970s and early 1980s, before his death in 1983. Drawn to the deep, emotional beauty of the natural world, he expressed these feelings in the beautiful close-ups and landscape views that illustrate this book.

Paul E. Knoop, Jr.

I met Paul Knoop thirty years ago. We were co-workers at Aullwood during the 1960s, where he was a naturalist-teacher, director of Aullwood Audubon Center, and finally education co-ordinator of Aullwood Audubon Center and Farm. Retired now near Hocking Hills in southeastern Ohio, Paul is still a renowned student of natural history. He is considered by his peers to be a leading naturalist in the Midwest. A native Daytonian who grew up near Aullwood, his enthusiasm for the outdoors influences all followers, old and young alike.

Paul's text is from the heart. It is from thirty-five years of experience as a naturalist at Aullwood, walking the trails, managing the land, teaching thousands of children and interpreting the natural world. It derives as well from his lifelong relationship with close friend and mentor Marie Aull.

Dane Mutter
Former director, Aullwood Children's Farm

Allan L. Horvath

On my early morning walks I used to encounter Allan Horvath. He was often sitting, sometimes lying, in the wet grass, just waiting for the right light for a photograph.
Marie Aull

Paul Knoop is a walking field-guide and a model for teaching so many different kinds of people, always retaining his sense of wonder at the natural world.
John Wilson
Aullwood environmental educator

Introduction

Since the early 1920s, when John and Marie Aull moved to their home in the woodland bordering the Stillwater River, the land, called Aullwood, has been open year-round to anyone seeking refreshment in the sea of flowers and beautiful vistas. Friends, strangers, young and old have sought the peaceful surroundings, developing an appreciation of nature.

A Place Called Aullwood is an adventure, exploring the evolution of a quiet valley through the dreams of two remarkable people.

Part A explores what the land was like millions of years before John Aull acquired the property. It tells of how Marie and John met and then settled in the valley.

Part B describes the plan Marie set in motion that opened the land permanently to the public, first creating the nature center and then preserving an adjoining farm.

Part C recounts a final, major challenge that threatened Aullwood's existence. It then goes on to celebrate Aullwood's diverse educational activities which have touched millions of lives by raising awareness, teaching environmental understanding, and increasing stewardship toward the Earth.

As Mike Shannon, a former Aullwood naturalist, once said, "Aullwood is a place where land and people get together to share in the process of living... a place to encounter dawn... probe a marsh... explore a farm... look across a tallgrass prairie... experience natural things. You have come at a good time."

Charity Krueger
director
Aullwood Audubon Center and Farm

A Place Called Aullwood
in Southwestern Ohio:

Its Flowers, Woodlands and Meadows
Photographic Essay
by Allan L. Horvath, PhD, APSA

Editor - Gail Horvath

Table of Contents

Ostrich fern

1. It's Ancient History!

450 Million Years Old!

The limestone rocks exposed along the banks of the Stillwater River tell us that the place we call Aullwood has a history stretching back at least 450 million years.

Once There Was an Ocean...

Because of their fossil imprints of ancient sea creatures, these rocks show us that once there was an ancient sea covering Aullwood.

With Millions of Creatures!

Millions of creatures lived in this warm shallow sea, their hard parts eventually becoming limestone rock when the sea retreated.

Good Soil

The limestone that the ancient sea left here created a rich soil, good for the growth of forest trees, wild flowers and other vegetation, which in turn provided calcium and magnesium to animals feeding on them.

Then There Were Glaciers...

Several glaciers have come here and gone, acting as giant bulldozers, pulverizing earth and rock, rounding hills, shredding trees and diverting streams.

The Last Glacier

The most recent ice mass came from northern Ohio 14,000 years ago and left behind large granite boulders along Wiles Creek, and rounded hillocks in fields and along Aullwood Road near Aullwood Garden.

Native Americans

Aullwood artifacts I've seen indicate that native Americans were here a few hundred years before European settlement.

Pioneer Village of Little York

Sometime before Europeans settled Dayton in 1795, a small pioneer village called Little York was established along the Stillwater River, near the present intersection of Meeker Road and Heathcliff.

Summers on the Stillwater

A hundred years later, many residents in the then bustling city of Dayton purchased summer cottages along the Stillwater River.

Daytonian John W. Aull was to purchase one such cottage along the Stillwater....

The Stillwater River is a natural treasure that the Dayton Canoe Club members enjoy on a regular basis. In recent years we have seen a resurgence in the water quality and the abundance of fish and wildlife there.
Dale Goubeaux
Dayton Canoe Club

Following pages:
Stillwater River near Aullwood >

7

Woods in autumn

Jean Smith

Aullwood Road, 1921

2. John Aull

A Weekend Retreat

Residing in downtown Dayton, businessman John Aull one day in 1907 followed a country road north of the city, beyond the village of Little York to a small wooded farm that contained a one-room cabin. He fell in love with the 150-acre farm along the Stillwater River and purchased it as a weekend retreat.

French and German Parents

John W. Aull was born March 27, 1866 to a French mother, Julia Gigler, a native of Hagerstown, Maryland, and a German father, Nicholas L. Aull. John had five sisters, Louisa, Catherine, Eva, Emma and Julia, and two brothers, William J. and Frank N.

Starting Young

John Aull attended Dayton public schools until the age of 14, when family finances obliged him to go to work early. He then joined a wholesale paper manufacturer, R.A. Rogers and Company.

The Aull Brothers

In 1882, John Aull's two older brothers, William J. and Frank N., founded a company to sell paper and paper boxes. John became a traveling salesman for the company in 1885 and was in charge of manufacturing by 1893.

A Successful Company

The company, Aull Brothers Paper and Box Company, moved several times to handle its growth, its final location a pie-shaped building still standing on Dutoit Street, where it employed 150 people by 1919. The company's main product was the gray or green florist box.

A Family Tragedy

In March, 1895, Will Aull, Sr., John's oldest brother and president of the Aull Brothers' company, went to Cincinnati with his wife, where they boarded the steamer The Longfellow, bound for New Orleans. The pilot's vision was obscured by fog and smoke, and the steamer crashed into a bridge pier and sank. Will Aull and his wife did not survive.

After the Tragedy

After Will's death, Frank became president and John

Wiles Creek in spring

John Aull and Stoddard-Dayton
in front of the Dayton Bicycle Club
20 W. Fourth Street, 1909

*One day Uncle John was
sitting in the passenger
seat of a Model-T while
Dad was cranking the
car to get it started.
Uncle John said,
'Careful, Ramy, you'll
break your arm.' And
sure enough, Dad broke
his arm cranking it once
more!*

John F. Aull, grand-nephew of
John and Marie Aull

treasurer of the paper and box company. In 1918, Frank moved to California. His interest was taken over by John, who became president, and Will Aull, Jr., the son of John's deceased brother.

Outdoorsman and Horseman

John Aull enjoyed travel and reading, but he most loved to be outdoors. He was an avid horseman. A grand-niece, Mary Aull Prugh, recalls, "I remember as a child learning to ride horseback at Uncle John's. Uncle John kept a horse at the farm in the barn, (where the Aullwood Center building is today) and let me ride it."

Bicycles

John Aull was a member of the Dayton Bicycle Club for more than 50 years. The group made Sunday bicycle runs to neighboring cities and was active in civic and charitable activities. The Bicycle Club was one of John's favorite places to meet with friends over a meal.

Automobiles

John was quite interested in the cars that were being built in Dayton in the early 1900s, but put off buying one until he had completely stopped drinking for six months. In 1909 he had kept his vow, and a friend who sold Stoddard-Daytons delivered one to him at the Bicycle Club and asked him to test-drive it from Dayton, Ohio to Daytona, Florida. It was a rugged and adventurous trip over wagon-rutted and rock-strewn roads that took twenty-one days one-way!

The Flood

Several years after John purchased the Aull farm, a natural disaster unparalleled in the area's history struck the Miami Valley. An unrelenting rain in March, 1913, coupled with frozen ground, caused the Great Miami River and its tributaries to overflow. Every city along the Great Miami River was inundated with flood waters: Dayton, Hamilton, Piqua... "My husband said that Dayton was almost destroyed by it," says Marie Aull. The waters of the Stillwater River, a tributary of the Great Miami north of Dayton, flooded the Aull farm and completely surrounded the small cabin on the hill.

John Aull and favorite horse Pansy

Indian grass and coneflower

Safe on the Hill
Because John Aull's house was in a high and dry location, people from Little York lived there until the flood waters receded.

Cleaning Up
Marie recalls, "Ethel Rike liked to tell how she didn't see her husband Fred for six weeks after the flood, because he had to go off to New York and get money to clean up and replace stock. He had just moved into the new Rike-Kumler store at Second and Main before the flood. You can't imagine how messy it was!" John helped organize a relief kitchen in Dayton that fed the men brought in to clean up flood debris.

Keeping Promises
Many people stranded in attics and on rooftops during the flood of 1913 made promises to prevent this kind of disaster from ever happening again. After the flood, the community kept its promises, led by John H.Patterson, president of the National Cash Register Company. John Aull was on the finance committee which raised the money within months, without benefit of state or federal funds, for an unprecedented local flood control project for the entire Miami River Valley. This flood control project would have ramifications for John Aull's land, and it would also have future ramifications for Aullwood Audubon Center and Farm.

Arthur Morgan
Hired to design the project was Arthur Morgan, a talented young engineer who was to make the flood control system innovative and world-famous. In later years, I had the opportunity to talk with Arthur Morgan. He was a gentle and humble man, interested in and knowledgeable about many things. He knew a lot about plants, trees and wildlife, and devoted his entire life to improving the human condition.

A Wonder!
The Miami Conservancy District was formed in 1915 and was the largest construction employer in the world at that time, with 2,000 people working on five dams, one for each stream. Construction began in 1918 and was completed in 1922. At the time, it was the most comprehensive flood control system in the nation, was the first to utilize the dry dam system (it had no moving parts), and the first to utilize an hydraulic jump (a kind of descending staircase) to slow water velocity

Along with the Aulls, the Miami Conservancy District has sought to preserve the natural integrity of this area, first under the Conservancy Park System, and today through its partnership with Five Rivers MetroParks.
P. Michael Robinette, RS
general manager, Miami
Conservancy District

Our company, Price Brothers, originally located in Michigan, did some work for the Conservancy District in 1916. We relocated to Dayton, working on the construction of the dams. Our family has been friends of the Aulls and the Conservancy ever since.
Marlay Price
Price Brothers Company

< Poppy

below each dam. The hydraulic jump had been tested in the swimming pool of Col. Edward Deeds, who with Charles F. Kettering and their company, Delco, had produced the electric self-starter, revolutionizing the automobile industry.

Morgan Place

Arthur Morgan's social thinking was ahead of his time. Each construction site had modern and sanitary housing for workers' families, its own school for children, free night school for adults, a mess hall, green space around the homes, and community associations for self-governing. At Englewood Dam, the housing area was called Morgan Place, though Morgan himself never lived there. Some homes from that time remain on the high ground near Main Street.

Englewood Dam

John Aull agreed to sell fifty acres of his farm property to the Miami Conservancy District so that Englewood Dam, the largest of the five dams, could be built. This permanently blocked his view of the Stillwater River to the north. "John was very interested in the dam. They used to call him the night watchman, because he would come back to the farm after work and see how things were going," says Marie.

John could not foresee that the Miami Conservancy District, the Dayton-Montgomery County Park District, which followed the establishment of the Conservancy District, and a tobacco-chewing judge would come to his future wife's and Aullwood's aid to protect them from a different kind of threat, commercial development, more than forty years later!

In John's immediate future was a trip to Alaska and a breath-taking introduction to Marie Sturwold, his future wife.

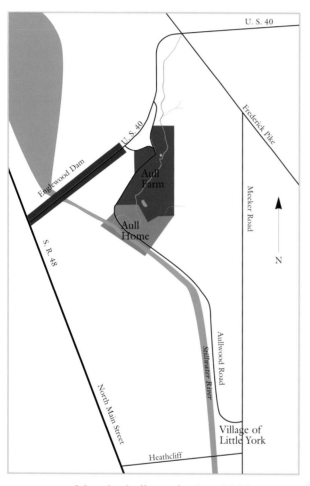

Map 1. Aullwood, circa 1923

Bloodroot >

3. Marie Sturwold

Dutchman's breeches remind me of my father. That's the first flower he taught me to identify.
Marie Aull

Run, Ma'am!

Marie Sturwold met John Aull in 1922. Her eyes sparkle when she relates the story. "A friend of my mother asked me to accompany her on a tour of Alaska," she recalls. "I was to meet her in Chicago, but when I arrived, the train for Alaska was already pulling out and there was my mother's friend waving frantically from the rear car. The porter asked, 'Can you run, ma'am?' As we caught up with the train, a tall, good-looking man reached down and helped to pull me aboard. And that was how I met John!"

A Family of Gardeners

Marie Sturwold was born in Cincinnati, January 8, 1897 to Anthony Sturwold and Rose Dickhaus Sturwold. She and her older sister Catherine were part of a family of gardeners. Her mother was famous for her flower garden, and her father had a vegetable garden. "I can remember going out to my grandfather's vegetable garden as a little girl. He would pull out a carrot and clean it and give it to me," she says. "And my grandmother had a very pretty garden. I remember her four o'clocks."

Nature Study

Despite her family's green thumb, Marie resisted gardening as a child. However, when she attended the University of Cincinnati, she took courses in botany, geology and bird study.

A Famous Teacher

During her college years, Marie was deeply influenced by one of her teachers, E. Lucy Braun, a noted botanist and forest ecologist. In later years, Dr. Braun remembered her student and sent Marie Aull seeds of the celandine poppy, a spectacular spring wildflower that I have admired in both the Aullwood Garden and Aullwood Center woodlands.

Courtship

During the month-long trip to Alaska, John and Marie became friends. They courted for the next year, with John traveling the bumpy road from Dayton to Cincinnati several days a week. Marie laughingly recalls that Ohio Governor "Jimmy Cox said he would make John put down a new road if he didn't stop wearing out the one between Dayton and Cincinnati!"

18   Marriage would soon solve the transportation problem for John and Marie.

Dutchman's breeches

Celandine poppy

Closed bottled gentian

Small pansy and cultivar

4. Gardening for Two

Let's Get Married!

Barely a year after they met, John Aull and Marie Sturwold decided to get married on June 23, 1923, despite the difference in their ages. Marie was 26 and John 57.

A Good Match

"John Aull was a large, well-proportioned man, over six feet tall, who was most affable, gentle and soft-spoken, reminding me of a big teddy bear," says Dr. Joseph Wilson, recalling John Aull fifty years later. "He was fun to live with," Marie says. Marie, small, attractive and the more romantic of the two, was his equal. "They were a good match for each other," says Mary Aull Prugh, "each very individualistic and unique."

Live in the Country?

Within months after their marriage, the couple decided to live year-round in the country north of Dayton, on John Aull's farm. This move raised some eyebrows, because "in those days one just didn't live in the country in the winter," says Marie.

The Farm

The Aull property continued to be farmed while John and Marie lived at the cabin. Crops were planted in what is now the prairie, and cattle and sheep grazed the property, including the woodland. A tenant farmer lived in the old stone farm house overlooking Wiles Creek, down the path from John and Marie. This house today is the residence of the director of Aullwood Audubon Center and Farm.

The House

Built in the 1890s, John's cabin was much more comfortable by the time he brought his bride there in 1923. He had remodeled and expanded the house, and built a garage and a swimming pool. "Uncle John really loved that house," recalls Mary Prugh. "I remember how proud he was of the animal figures in the small stained glass windows, made here in Dayton."

The Reading Room Picture Window

The only major addition to the house after their marriage was the small reading/viewing room, a place that proved to be Marie's favorite spot.

This garden is the result of sixty years of trial and error.
Marie Aull

Photograph by Ben Jakobowski

Stained-glass window in Aull home, Aullwood Garden

21

Pasque flower

Driveway, Aullwood Garden

Marie recalls, "I wanted a large window to view the outdoors, but the contractor told me he couldn't do it. 'Besides,' he said, 'it's in bad taste.' 'Well,' I said, 'I'm sorry, but that's what I want!'"

Let's Garden!

Marie Aull recalls the decision to start a wildflower garden. "John loved to ride horseback. I played golf before I was married but he didn't care much for golf and I didn't care for horseback riding so we decided we would grow wildflowers."

Nurturing the Valley

The land at the place called Aullwood, having previously been farmed, needed a lot of careful, loving attention. With the help of the tenant farmer and an occasional workman, John and Marie Aull spent the next several decades carefully building and nurturing the small valley along the Stillwater River.

A Few Flowers

"John fenced off the adjoining seventy acres of farm, keeping the cattle and sheep from the woodland property surrounding our cabin. Suddenly a few flowers appeared. We spent weekends going around the countryside finding flowers that we could bring in and get started," recounts Marie.

Flowers, Flowers, Flowers

The streams had been re-channeled and quaint stone bridges built over them following the devastating 1913 flood. Now John and Marie created wild and cultivated flower gardens along the woodland borders and stream terraces. They planted wildflowers, including hepaticas, Dutchman's breeches and celandine poppies, along borders and in the old growth woodland. They carefully placed many thousands of daffodils, spring aconites, hellebores, hostas and old-fashioned hyacinths in the rich, woodland soil.

Visitors

From the start, they encouraged visitors at the garden. "John would say, 'These things don't belong to us. We must pass them on to the next generation,'" says Marie. "It amuses me now to see this kind of thinking being propounded as innovative, when John felt that way, considering us custodians, back in the 1920s."

One spring while enjoying Aullwood Garden, I asked Marie how she kept out the dandelions. Her reply was, "We just dug them up, day after day, year after year, until they all gave up!"
Harry Butler
American Rock Garden Society

Aullwood has touched our community with a sense of place. From the time John and Marie first welcomed visitors to their garden, the natural beauty and people of this place have helped anchor us all in these busy times.
Doug Horvath
Aullwood environmental educator

Following pages: Back lawn and house rock garden, Aullwood Garden

>

Virginia bluebell

Garden Club

Shortly after her marriage, Marie was encouraged by Katherine Talbott, a friend of John Aull and the founder and president of the Dayton chapter of the Garden Club of America, to join the organization. At annual meetings of the national organization, Marie and John would often visit beautiful gardens around the country. (Katherine Talbott's husband, H.E. Talbott, had a construction company which was involved in the Miami Conservancy project. A son and great-grandson would later become Secretary of the Air Force and Deputy Secretary of State, respectively.)

Interested in Aviation

John Aull was very interested in airplanes and in 1924 worked on one of the committees at the first air show in Dayton, the International Air Races, chaired by Frederick B. Patterson. John had already met Orville and Wilbur Wright and had pulled the Wright Brothers' plane on occasion to help get it started. "John met Jimmy Doolittle and other great pilots of the time, because they were stationed during the war at McCook Field," recalls Marie. (In World War I, the flying field for Dayton was McCook Field, located in the vicinity of the Royal Z Dayton, formerly McCook's Bowling Alley, on Keowee Street. Wright-Patterson Air Force Base did not yet exist.)

The Depression

The Depression was hard on John Aull's paper box company. "John and the other executives took no pay for two years, so that the line workers could keep their jobs, doing public works projects," says Kevin Kepeler, Aullwood Garden park manager.

The Rock Garden

The rock garden on the slope behind the house was created as a result of John Aull asking a young man in Little York to haul down some rocks if he had any slow days while John and Marie were on one of their trips. "When we came home after six weeks, there were mountains of rock back here, and we had to build a rock garden then, whether we wanted to or not," Marie recalls.

Virginia Bluebells

"I bought a hundred Virginia bluebells for the rock garden and planted them, but I realized they would take over the rock garden, so I transplanted some in the woods," says Marie.

We have nicknamed Jean Woodhull and Marie Aull "our garden gurus." Our special name for Marie is "our natural treasure."
Mary Martin, Garden Club of Dayton historian

The Four Seasons Garden Club has great respect and affection for Marie Aull. We frequently work on different aspects of the same gardening projects together.
Jane Olt
Four Seasons Garden Club

In the spring, mertensia virginica paves the hill-sides and woods of Aullwood with thousands and thousands of azure blossoms, as if the heavens had fallen there. The acres of blue began with one hundred plants Marie Aull set into the ground years ago. That is Aullwood to me.
Roz Young, columnist
Dayton Daily News

Blue-eyed Mary

Bleeding hearts

The Woodland Swimming Pool

John used to take a swim in the spring-fed woodland pool every morning. "Our cook used to say, 'Mr. John, I wish you wouldn't holler so when you get in that pool. It makes me shiver-r-r-r!' Well, I tried swimming in that cold water once or twice and then that was the end of it for me," laughs Marie.

Family

John and Marie had no children, but they did have relatives. Marie's mother would come from Cincinnati for weeks at a time. And married brothers and sisters on both sides would come with their families.

My husband's favorite flower was the blue-eyed Mary.
Marie Aull

I used to walk to Aullwood with my girl-friends in the seventh and eighth grades. We would look for snakes there and see how many we could find.
Patricia Aull Hay, grand-niece of John and Marie Aull

Woodland swimming pool

Yellow lady's slipper

John's Heart
In 1936, John Aull had a severe heart attack, which forced him to drastically change his lifestyle. During this difficult period, doctors ordered him to spend more time at Aullwood and less time at his business.

Selling the Company
After a second attack in 1945, John contacted Robert C. Neff, who was running the Gebhart Folding Box Co., and sold his company to Gebhart.

Watching the Sun Set
"Aullwood was John's haven. He would go out in the garden and do small jobs. We would walk by the hour. We would sit and watch the sunset. To John there was no such thing as an ordinary sunset," Marie says.

Soon Marie would have to watch sunsets alone.

I have bulbs and plants in my garden that Marie started giving me in the early 1960s. We'd get down on our hands and knees and dig them out together. All the while, I was learning about propagation, care of plants, botanical names, etc. Marie is a true horticulturist. Her love of nature is truly contagious.
Ruth Mead, civic leader

I would say that Marie is the Johnny Appleseed of flowers. I remember a typical phone message from her: "It's 5:30 a.m., Sue, and I've got iris to share with you!" Hospice of Dayton currently reflects Marie's generosity (horticultural and otherwise).
Sue Jackson
Commercial Foliage

Spangle gras

Canada burnet and horsetail

Purple coneflower

Prairie pattern in winter

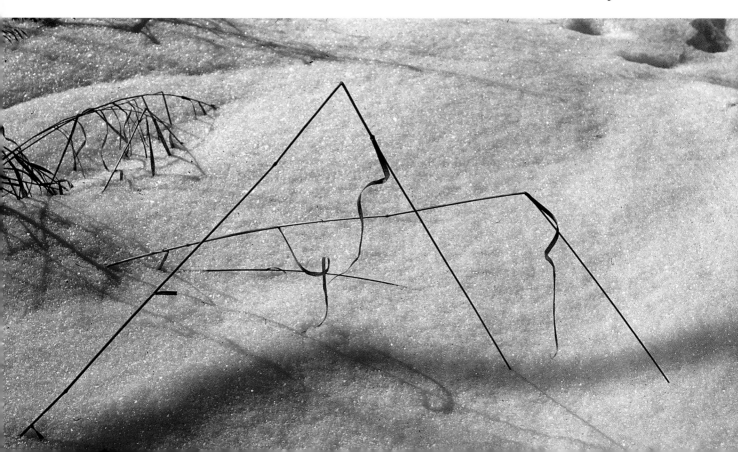

5. Creating Aullwood Audubon Center

Without John

After John Aull died on January 1, 1955, at the age of 89, Marie had to decide what to do with the farmland that had been fenced off from the property around the Aull home and garden.

What to Do with the Aull Farm?

Marie asked the National Audubon Society in 1956 if it would be interested in the property, after her death, as a plant and wildlife sanctuary. John H. Baker, president of the National Audubon Society, responded that he would like the property, but suggested that Marie give the land right away, to "have the fun of seeing people enjoy all its benefits."

Marie's Answer

Marie Aull accepted Baker's advice and donated the seventy-acre farm property to the Audubon Society in 1956, keeping the thirty-acre Aullwood garden and home for herself. The Aull farmland would become an environmental education center called Aullwood Audubon Center.

The Weary Land

The task of healing the land and bringing back what was native to the area would be an ongoing endeavor. Prior to 1800, this land was completely forested. But settlers seeking new farmland removed most of the large trees, leaving only a few original oaks and sycamores and smaller second-growth trees. Grazing cattle and sheep eliminated most of the woodland wildflowers. By 1956, when Marie donated the property to the National Audubon Society, the land had the look of an intensely used farm. Livestock trails traversed the stream and wooded hillsides, and fences abounded everywhere. Natural habitat areas had been abused or entirely lost.

Back to School

Marie Aull spent the time just prior to the completion of the Aullwood Audubon Center "going to school." She visited Audubon Centers in Connecticut, California and Wisconsin. At the latter she met a specialist in teaching natural history, Dorothy Treat, who

Aullwood respects children, it uses the discovery approach and lets the natural world do the teaching, all the while having fun.
Dianna Ullery
former naturalist, Aullwood
Audubon Center and Farm

Highbush cranberry

33

was to have a profound effect on her understanding of outdoor education. Marie Aull says, "I was enormously impressed with the way Dorothy could transfer her enthusiasm for natural things even to older people."

Challenges for Aullwood Audubon Center's First Director

Thomas P. McElroy, Jr. arrived as managing director of Aullwood Audubon Center on May 1, 1957. McElroy, an experienced wildlife management expert and author of The New Handbook of Attracting Birds, had the daunting challenge of transforming the former Aull farm into a community environmental education center and restoring the damaged or lost wildlife communities wherever possible.

Transformation from Farm to Environmental Education Center

Working as a volunteer with McElroy at Aullwood from 1957 until I officially joined the staff in 1959 as a teacher-naturalist, I had an opportunity to observe the transformation first-hand. It was an intensely productive time, which resulted in dramatic changes to the land. We removed a large barn and numerous outbuildings, built several homes for staff and constructed a new headquarters building on the site of the old barn. A trail system was laid out reaching into the heart of diverse habitat areas: stream, woodland, meadow, pond, and marsh. Wildflowers were reintroduced to the bare, wooded hillsides, mostly from Marie's garden: Virginia bluebells, Dutchman's breeches, trilliums, celandine poppies and numerous other species. We created aquatic areas such as muskrat marsh, bluegill pond and others, where bull and green frogs, turtles and watersnakes, migrating ducks and shorebirds now abound or the rare spotted salamander now breeds. An elevated trail was made through a wooded swamp, where skunk cabbage and marsh marigold can be seen.

Dedication of Aullwood Center

After only six months of work, the Aullwood Audubon Center was ready to be officially dedicated to the Dayton community on November 2, 1957, largely due to McElroy's efforts. Dorothy Treat was the first education director, and after Tom McElroy left in 1960, she would become Aullwood's director.

A lot of my philosophy of life was formed at Aullwood. That place is a part of my whole being. I really miss it and I continually think about it.
Paul Knoop

My mother taught in Oakwood in the 1960s. She used to take her classes to Aullwood Audubon Center.
Willa Marie Magner

I love the flowers and I love the bugs.
second-grader Emily Allen

As a young intern there, possibly the first one, I rehabilitated injured birds. This direct one-on-one experience turned me on to birds.
John McNeely, author of Veedor, the Condor

Marie Aull and Paul Knoop
photographer unknown

Meadow foxtail

Butterfly weed

An Outdoor Classroom

Within months after the Center's dedication, teachers and their students were streaming to Aullwood to participate in a new experience, a high-quality outdoor classroom where students could become more perceptive and sensitive to the world around them and ultimately better stewards of the Earth's resources.

The Tallgrass Prairie

In the spring of 1960, we began work on re-creating a bit of the original prairie vegetation of Ohio, the tallgrass prairie. More than one hundred species of prairie grasses and wildflowers now abound on the ten-acre parcel, presenting a spectacular display in late July and August. This area is considered one of Ohio's best examples of restored tallgrass prairie.

Dorothy Treat Dies

When Dorothy Treat died in 1964, the Aullwood staff and Marie were devastated. We had lost a great teacher. I was then named director of Aullwood Audubon Center, and held that post for fourteen years.

Model for Other Nature Centers

As one of the first nature centers in the Midwest, Aullwood became a model for other nature centers, both locally, such as the Brukner Nature Center in Troy, and the Cincinnati Nature Center, as well as around the country, such as Seven Ponds Nature Center in Dryden, Michigan.

Within only a year of the dedication of the Aullwood Center, the threat of commercial development on neighboring property appeared, the first of two major threats to Aullwood's existence.

Taking kids on the trails, through the wetwoods and skunk cabbage. On to the prairie where the giant bluestem is way over their heads. Then back to the Center area to have them feel a touch-me-not come to life in their hands. Kids discovering nature. That's Aullwood.

Mac Reich, volunteer trail guide, Aullwood Audubon Center and Farm

In the fall of the year, I like to take the children's groups out to the tower, especially when the wind is blowing, because the tall prairie grass looks like the waves of a sea.

Jim Quinn
volunteer trail guide, Aullwood Audubon Center and Farm

I remember visiting Marie at Aullwood in the late 1950s with Stanley M. Rowe, when the Cincinnati Nature Center was being planned, using Aullwood as a model.

Helen Black
honorary board member
Cincinnati Nature Center

Aullwood is a premier environmental education center of the National Audubon Society.

Steve Sedam
Great Lakes Regional Vice-President, National Audubon Society

Big bluestem grass

Tall coreopsis

Spotted touch-me-not

Exploring the trail

Following pages: Running in the woods

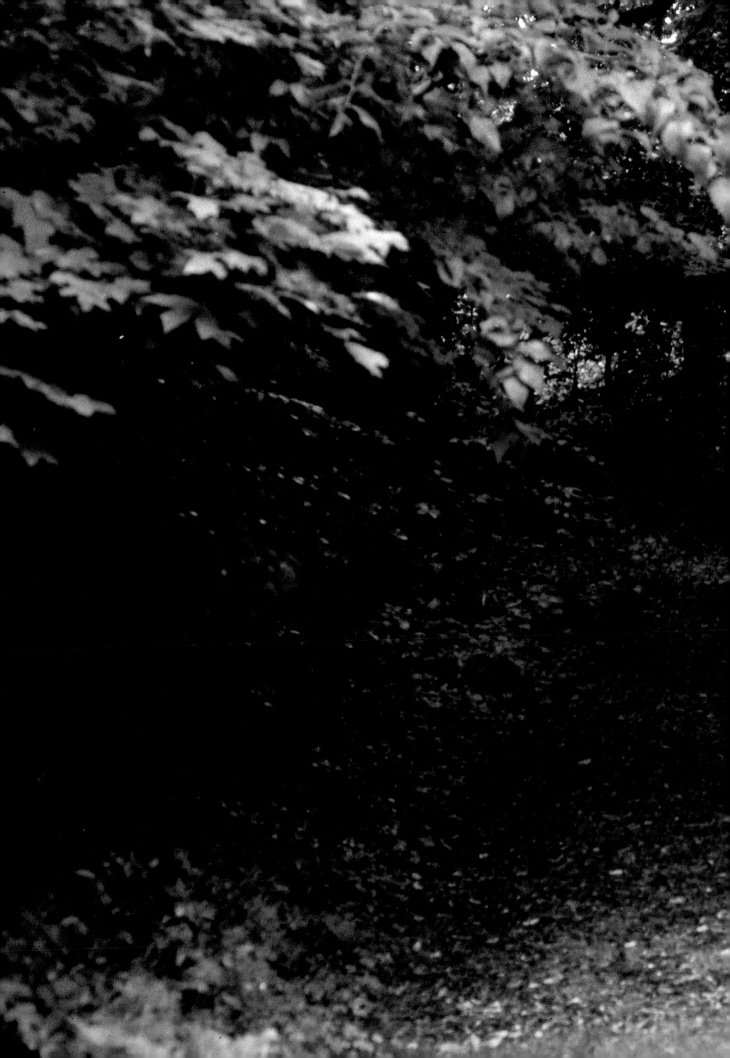

I remember how much my husband Gene and I enjoyed taking our grandchildren around the Aullwood Children's Farm with Marie Aull in the mid-1960s.

Virginia Kettering, civic leader

My mother, Lenore Thomas, was a close friend of Marie Aull and worked as a volunteer with Paul Knoop. I have happy memories of Marie and her place. My son and I recently took his two daughters to Dayton so they could know Marie and her lovely grounds as well.

Carolyn Talbot Hoagland

When we pass through Dayton, we often detour and drive through the farm gate and down the lane of maple saplings, now sizable trees, that I planted with a friend in 1974.

David J. Sammons, former teacher-naturalist, Aullwood Audubon Farm

Photograph by Charity Krueger

Aullwood barn and buildings

6. Creating the Aullwood Children's Farm

Building Homes
When homes are built, streams and springs which feed them are always destroyed during the construction process. Wiles Creek, which flows through Aullwood Center and into Aullwood Garden, starts from springs on neighboring property that was the 120-acre George Antrim farm.

First Threat of Nearby Commercial Development
About a year after Aullwood's dedication, the first threat of nearby commercial development occurred. The Antrim farm was going to be sold and subdivided. This development would have destroyed the springs which feed Wiles Creek. The creek would have become a dry creek bed, no longer able to support plants and wildlife.

Buying the Antrim Farm
Marie went to visit the owner, Mrs. Antrim, and convinced her to sell the farm, promising not to develop it and guaranteeing her lifetime residency there. With the purchase of the Antrim farm in 1960, the first threat of development on neighboring property was averted.

What about a Working Farm for Children?
Marie contacted the National Audubon Society for its support of a working farm for children on the Antrim property. Though a new venture for the National Audubon Society, Mrs. Aull's gift was accepted and Aullwood Children's Farm was dedicated on October 7, 1962.

Dr. George Graff, Director
Under the leadership of Dr. George Graff, who was director at the farm from early 1963 to summer of that year, there was immediate community support for the Children's Farm. A local Friends group raised funds for a classroom addition to the main barn, a sugarhouse, springhouse and other buildings.

Organic Farming
Fruit trees, a wild berry patch, bee-hives and some black walnut trees were a part of the Antrim Farm and remain today. Only organic materials are used on the farm for pest and weed control and fertilizer.

42

Photograph by Charity Krueger

Dane Mutter

From August, 1963, to March, 1967, Dane Mutter, an Ohio State University Wildlife Management graduate, directed the Aullwood Children's Farm.

The Thomas Building

In 1964 Lenore Thomas of Dayton provided funds to erect the Thomas Building, the farm's main headquarters and meeting area.

Farm Staff

At first the farm staff consisted of the farm director, who resided in the old Antrim home, and the resident farmer, along with a few weekend volunteers. Gradually teachers were added.

The Sugarbush

The farm includes a sugarbush, a ten-acre beech/maple woodland where maple trees are tapped and sap is boiled into maple syrup every winter, a favorite activity of Aullwood staff and visitors.

Sugaring off

My favorite thing is when I tapped a maple tree and the sap ran like a leaky faucet and then I watched as they made maple syrup from this sap.

Susan Siehl, volunteer, Aullwood Audubon Center and Farm

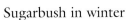

Sugarbush in winter

Even after thirty years of working with the herb garden at Aullwood Farm, there's still something new to learn.

Jan Landefeld, president
Greenview Garden Club

We're grateful to the Aullwood staff for their encouragement, enthusiasm and help in 1973 in starting the Learning Tree Project to provide hands-on learning experiences in a traditional farm setting.

Sally Keyes, co-founder
Learning Tree

There are tons of animals there.

first-grader Katrina Edwards

Restoring the Land

The land at the Children's Farm was restored. Wooded areas, including the sugarbush, were carefully managed, and fence rows were improved for wildlife.

The Herb Garden

In 1966, the Greenview Garden Club built the herb garden and the herb house to demonstrate and share with others the usefulness and beauty of herbs. The club has continued to maintain both.

A Model Farm

With groundwork laid by Graff and Mutter, and under the able leadership of Jack Wood, who joined the staff in August, 1967, Aullwood Children's Farm became a model for farm education in the Midwest. Many thousands of children have come to experience a working farm at Aullwood. They have been able to look at a cow, hear a rooster crow, feel a warm egg, walk through a field of growing corn, and watch sap drip from a maple tree.

The years brought new farm buildings. Soon the time would also be ripe for a new, closer relationship between the two organizations.

Photograph by Charity Krueger

Dee Dee and May

44

Aullwood draws some of the most kind, caring, and inquisitive people I've ever met to a common place, to enjoy the natural experience of encountering the outdoors.
Jennifer Lokai
Aullwood environmental educator

The invitation to become a volunteer trail guide at Aullwood came at a difficult time in my life, but the staff's encouragement enabled me to teach the children's groups, and to experience sunshine and laughter again.
Ann King

Fungi

Common milkweed pod

The ideal place for environmental learning to take place is the outdoors.
John Ritzenthaler
Aullwood environmental educator

I had long heard of Aullwood before my work brought me to Dayton, providing the opportunity for me to experience first-hand its natural beauty.
Mike McKenzie
international businessman

7. Combining the Children's Farm and Aullwood Center

Consolidation into One Unit

In 1978, the National Audubon Society wanted to close Aullwood Children's Farm, now called Aullwood Audubon Farm, for financial reasons. It was persuaded instead to consolidate the two units. This eliminated duplication of effort, enhanced the cooperative spirit between Aullwood staff and community members, and cut operating expenses. With Jack Wood as director and me as education director, the combined unit, now called Aullwood Audubon Center and Farm, moved into the 1980s in a strengthened position.

Volunteers

Diana Ullery, naturalist at the Aullwood Audubon Farm and later the combined unit, recruited more volunteers to enable us to give the same number of programs with only half the staff. Volunteers grew from a handful to one hundred, and we eventually relied on them to provide much of the teaching.

Interns

Interns came from all over the world to be trained at Aullwood Audubon Center and Farm, giving additional assistance, and necessitating remodeling some of the farm buildings for more housing.

Charity Krueger

In 1982, Charity Krueger arrived as director of the Aullwood Audubon Center and Farm, bringing with her a special dedication to creating innovative education programs. Under her leadership in 1986, and with the support of a strong Friends of Aullwood board of directors, Aullwood Audubon Center and Farm was able to become financially self-sufficient.

The Barn Is Burning!

On the morning of June 18, 1987, the big barn at the Aullwood Farm burned to the ground. The 125-year-old barn was an historical landmark and its loss was devastating to the local community.

I enjoy the prairie, the wetwoods, the bluegill pond and the barn. All of these places provide beauty and peace.
Charity Krueger
director, Aullwood Audubon
Center and Farm

Just yesterday, I saw a fox in the middle of the pasture. And we see coyotes, and lots of owls, hawks, and ground hogs.
Bob Grimes, Aullwood farmer

The cows were big and some of their hair was curly.
first-grader Daniel Kemper

Photograph by Duryea Morton

Sow and piglets

46

A New Barn

Charity sought community support to replace the barn with an historic barn built in 1889. Within only one year, with a substantial contribution from Sally Reahard, granddaughter of John Aull's brother Will Aull, Sr., an almost exact replica of the original barn was in place.

Airport Prairie

In 1994, the Dayton International Airport asked Aullwood Audubon Center and Farm to manage 150 acres of airport land adjacent to Aullwood and Five Rivers MetroParks land. This land was re-planted as a new prairie and named the Paul E. Knoop, Jr. Prairie Preserve, much to my great joy. This meant that Aullwood Audubon Center and Farm now managed 350 acres, including five miles of trails, through prairie, meadow, mature woods, wetlands and organic farm fields. How it had grown from the original seventy acres I first saw back in 1957!

Aullwood Audubon Center and Farm demanded much of Marie's time during this period. However, Marie still had a garden to manage....

Snake skin

I like Aullwood's forest because of all the trees.
second-grader Ian Harker

Crossing Wiles Creek

8. Donating the Garden

Mrs. Aull's Garden

All the while that Marie was supervising the development of Aullwood Audubon Center and later the Aullwood Children's Farm, she also continued to manage her garden, often just called "Mrs. Aull's garden."

A Gift to the New Park District

In 1963, Marie Aull, Jean Woodhull, and Dayton Journal Herald editor Glenn Thompson played major roles in the creation of the Dayton-Montgomery County Park District. The park district later changed its name to Five Rivers MetroParks. In 1977, Marie Aull decided to donate her house, her thirty-acre garden and a maintenance endowment to the new park district, with the provision that she be able to reside on the property as long as she lived.

Watching over the Garden

Marie continued to direct the work of the gardeners after the donation of Aullwood Garden to the Park District. The gardener lived in the house that Marie had had built nearby on Aullwood Road. "When a new path and bridge were to be built from the parking lot to the Garden in the late 1980s, Marie was quite involved with the details, making sure that everything would be done right," recalls Ted Soptelean, former park district staff person in charge of the project.

Do You Know Mrs. Aull?

Despite the help of gardeners, Marie could not resist working in the garden herself, even at age 90. Marie laughs and says, "Sometimes someone would come in the garden and ask me if I knew Mrs. Aull. And I would just say, 'Well, I guess I do.' I never identified myself. I guess they wondered why a little old woman would have to support herself working on her hands and knees like that!"

Other Interests

Marie would often attend the ballet, the Dayton Philharmonic, and the opera with friends. She read voraciously in her sun room/study, kept up with current events, and took the time to support many causes, particularly those involving children and the environment. She lobbied successfully for the designation of the Stillwater River as a state scenic river. She was an

I remember working in Mrs. Aull's garden in 1987 and being thrilled at hearing a pileated woodpecker for the first time in many years.

Dave Knoop, former gardener
Aullwood Garden

In 15 years of working in Mrs. Aull's garden, I've learned that no two years are alike.

Lynn Millikin
gardener, Aullwood Garden

I wouldn't be the gardener I am today if it weren't for Mrs. Aull. And my knees will never be the same either!

Don Brumbaugh, former gardener, Aullwood Garden

I consider working with Marie my master gardening course.

Pat Gilbert, gardener to Mrs. Aull

We all love Aullwood. We learned gardening from Marie and now all four of our children love gardening. She is a great mentor and great friend!

Jean Woodhull, civic leader

Hepatica, Marie Aull's favorite flower

One night after an evening at the Dayton Philharmonic, Marie said to me, "Why don't we take a walk through the garden?" I hesitated. What could we possibly see at night? "My dear," she said, "the world of night has its own nocturnal creatures and flowers and fragrances." With these words, she changed my life.

Leonard Sweet, former president
United Theological Seminary

active Garden Club of Dayton member since shortly after its founding in 1922, and gave tours of her garden and special programs for many garden clubs in the area.

A Night under the Stars

One fall afternoon in 1985, Marie Aull went out walking alone near her home. She tripped and fell into Wiles Creek, breaking her hip. Realizing that no one was around, she was able to pull herself out of the creek and covered herself with leaves to keep warm. Knowing that the gardener would be coming in the morning and would find her, Marie spent that night outdoors nestled under the leaves, "enjoying the stars and the moon," as she later recalled. And after a period of recovery, she walked once again in her garden....

The story of John and Marie Aull and the place they called Aullwood is an ongoing story and it is many stories. One of the stories is about the fight against encroaching commercial development.

Daffodils, Aullwood Garden

9. The Englewood-Aullwood Complex and the Tobacco-chewing Judge

Fighting to Protect the Environment

Aullwood had to ward off serious threats to its existence. Purchasing the Antrim property and creating the Aullwood Children's Farm had averted the first such threat. Dane Mutter recounts the following story of the second fight to protect Aullwood's environment.

Englewood/Aullwood Complex Master Plan

"When the Dayton-Montgomery County Park District was created in 1963, Mrs. Aull and the staff at Aullwood asked the district's help in providing a buffer from possible development by purchasing land around Aullwood. These discussions resulted in the Englewood/Aullwood Complex Master Plan, where Englewood refers to the Miami Conservancy's Englewood Dam and not the city of Englewood.

A Shopping Center next to Aullwood?

"The threat of development was real. The owner of land to the east of Aullwood along Meeker Road planned to build a house and/or a small shopping center there. Located on the site is the county's biggest spring, whose waters flow into the woods above Marie's house and empty into Wiles Creek in Aullwood Garden. Development would destroy the spring, a sewage-treatment plant would be needed for the development site, there would be salty water run-offs from parking lots.... It would be disastrous for Aullwood.

Land Acquisition Plan

"The Englewood/Aullwood Plan called for acquisition and preservation of lands within an area bordered by the Miami Conservancy District's Englewood Dam to the north, Meeker Road to the east, Interstate 70 to the south, and west to the Stillwater River. Once completed, this would surround the Aullwood facility with park land. Dayton-Montgomery County taxpayers approved a modest levy in 1965. With this and a gift from Mrs. Aull and Eugene Kettering, the park district began its land acquisition program. The first purchase was a twenty-eight acre tract of land on Meeker Road.

Spring pond in winter

Wild black cherry tree

Negotiations for Meeker Road Land

"In 1966 the park district began negotiations to purchase additional Meeker Road land slated for development. The owner showed no interest in selling and later refused to discuss it any further. The park district board of commissioners was forced to seek the land through the power of eminent domain.

A Coming Showdown

"Early in the litigation process a showdown occurred. While teaching Saturday morning classes at Aullwood Farm, I heard loud engines running in the direction of the Meeker Road land. After finishing classes, I called Paul Knoop at Aullwood Center. Knoop had also heard what seemed to be tractors and we decided to investigate. Meeting along the fence row between Aullwood and the adjacent property, we observed three large bulldozers rapidly clearing the hillside of small trees and shrubs and pushing the debris into rows.

Calling the Law

"Knoop immediately called J. Richard (Dick) Lawwill, director of the park district. Rapid action followed. Park district attorney Paul Lacouture was called and he hurriedly wrote a motion for a restraining order and rushed to the home of Common Pleas Judge Carl Kessler. Kessler, dressing for a political dinner, signed the order and told Lacouture to let him know if he needed help.

Chased by a Bulldozer

"Lacouture delivered a copy to the owner's home, then hurried to the Meeker Road site to serve the restraining order to the equipment operators. They refused to stop. "A family member of the property owner appeared with a shotgun and ordered Lacouture off the property. Then a bulldozer operator chased Lacouture! Undaunted, Lacouture returned to the judge's home and asked for help. 'I think Kessler was glad to get out of his dinner clothes and into jeans and western boots,' commented Lacouture.

The Tobacco-chewing Judge

"The judge mouthed a quantity of chewing tobacco as he and Lacouture headed back to the Meeker Road site. Approaching the group in the field, Kessler began, 'I'm an officer of the court and I have an order for you to stop this equipment....You better damned well obey!' Expressing a fair amount of tobacco juice, he added, 'Anyone else who gets on a dozer will be an overnight guest of "Beno" Keiter. OK?' (Bernard Keiter was then Montgomery County Sheriff.)

A Calm Aftermath

"The remainder of that afternoon on the hillside above Aullwood, we could hear white-throat sparrows, woodpeckers and other small birds as they inspected the downed trees. Crows scratched in the moist, disturbed soil, accompanied by a flock of migrating robins searching for worms. The dozers had been silenced.

"In due time, the counter-lawsuit was settled in favor of the park district, a jury decided the true market value of the Meeker Road land, and the land, now called Big Spring Area, was finally acquired."

After several other land purchases nearby, the Aullwood facility was totally surrounded by park land, both Dayton-Montgomery County Park District land and Miami Conservancy District land, and was secure from the threat of commercial development. Let us take a moment to enjoy the place that has been so earnestly restored and protected for the future by so many people.

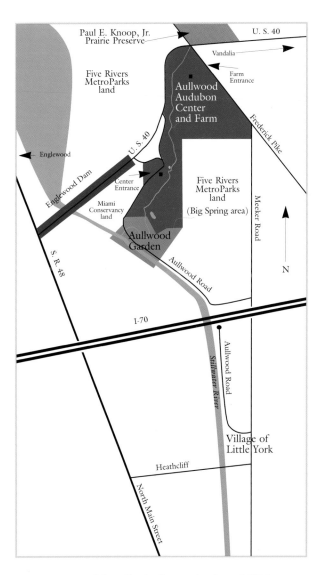

Map 2. Aullwood, circa 1994

White oak leaf

53

Aullwood Center building

Walking the trails

10. A Walk Through Aullwood Audubon Center

A Good Day to Explore

The day is warm and sunny: a perfect time to explore outdoors. Excitement shows on the children's faces as I invite them into Aullwood Center's Discovery Room.

The Discovery Room

The children handle some of the box turtles and non-venomous snakes. They scatter about and become involved in hands-on exhibits about honey bees, water turtles, and how plants are pollinated. They learn about wild animal tracks, a deer skeleton, insect homes, and forest ecology.

Be Alert!

Heading out the trail door, I hand each child a small magnifying lens which can be used to examine small objects close-up. I tell them to be alert: to look, to listen, to feel, and to smell, and, most important of all, to ask questions.

Glacial Rocks

Near the stream, large glacial rocks attract attention. Children touch and examine them with magnifiers. They ask, "Why are they so big? Where did they come from? What makes this one sparkle?"

The Stream

We cross the stream together on stepping stones and the children discover it is a neat experience. They find the crystal clear water to be very cold as they explore for water sow bugs, caddisflies and mayflies. They look up to admire the old sycamore tree overhanging the stream; its big limbs are white as snow against the blue sky. A sharp-eyed child notices honey bees passing in and out of a hole high in the sycamore. We've found a bee tree!

The Trail

On up the trail a giant, old white oak tree attracts attention as it has a large natural cavity at its base. Each child in turn crawls into the opening and stands up inside the tree. How many people have experienced the dark interior of an ancient oak tree?

The Meadow

On ahead in the meadow, children get on their hands and knees in the thick, unmowed grass and search for the well-worn trails of meadow voles. They find numerous trails, as well as open burrows that lead to underground living quarters. Rabbit droppings attract attention and the children examine and discuss them.

The Pine Woods

Approaching the pine woods, the children find the feathered remains of a dead cardinal. They fondle the feathers and admire their structure and color. In the pine woods, the children lie down, close their eyes and soak up the goodness of this special place.

Blue Gill Pond

On the return trip, the children pass blue gill pond, where they scatter along the edge and look for water animals and tracks. They startle a garter snake and it hurries to escape into the tall grass. The snake is captured and the children touch and handle it before releasing it back to the meadow.

An Exhilarating Experience

We return to the building somewhat tired and hungry but exhilarated, and we promise to go on another day to visit Aullwood Farm and its many animals and habitats.

But now, we want to experience the calm, simple beauty of the neighboring Aullwood Garden, site of the Aull homestead.

I found wild onions.
first-grader Lindsay Albert

I especially liked leading third- and fourth-graders in the fresh snow, finding footprints of skunk, rabbit, raccoon, and possum and having the children tell stories about them.
Byron Layman, Jr.
former Aullwood naturalist

Sometimes, if they are very quiet, the children are able to see deer in the woods.
Doug Horvath, Aullwood environmental educator

Rabbit tracks in snow

Following pages:
Wiles Creek in winter

11. A Visit to Aullwood Garden

Follow the Gravel Path

Leaving our cars in the small parking area for visitors to Aullwood Garden, we enter the gate and follow a gravel path along the nearby Stillwater River.

Red Marks the Spot

Just a few feet from the gate stands a 250-year-old bur oak tree that experienced the historic 1913 flood. I point out a red marker, placed twenty feet up on the trunk to indicate the 1913 high water mark, and the group imagines how the area looked back then.

At the Wooden Bridge

Just a few feet farther along the gravel path, the group pauses on the recently built arched wooden bridge that crosses Wiles Creek. From the bridge we view the clear, cold water of Wiles Creek and experience the nearby floodplain forest. This small stream starts as a trickle in the hills above Aullwood, picking up water from tiny hillside seeps which transform it into a wider creek along its meandering path through the garden to the Stillwater River.

Front Garden Lawn

Crossing Aullwood Road, we pass through the garden gate that opens into the heart of the garden. Large forest trees surround the expansive front lawn and beds of wild and cultivated flowers sweep in graceful curves along the lawn edge of nearby Wiles Creek. The quiet beauty of the garden envelops us.

Across the Stone Bridge

Just ahead, across the stone bridge, a rustic, brown sign posted on a chinquapin oak tree states simply, "This is a valley where nothing ever happens, where people simply live, where there is sun and slow peacefulness of day following day."

The Aull Homestead

We look up and see the Aull home, nestled on a hill in the center of the garden. Vines cluster on the weathered stone chimney and along one end of the enclosed porch, while forest trees lean gently over the roof.

I've visited a lot of gardens around the world, but Mrs. Aull's garden is a world-class garden in every respect.
Bob Siebenthaler, chairman of the board, Siebenthaler Nurseries

Oh-h-h-h! This is so-o-o beautiful! I want a garden like this some day.
seven-year-old Michelle Forgues

One of my favorite times in Aullwood Garden is winter time, because the garden's true structure can be clearly seen.
Kevin Kepeler, park manager
Aullwood Garden

It is with great pride that we offer this wonderful Aullwood Garden to the people of the Montgomery County community to enjoy true beauty.
Marvin Olinsky
director, Five Rivers MetroParks

58

Front lawn, Aullwood Garden

Aull home, Aullwood Garden

Rose bud

Marie's spirit permeates all that is at Aullwood, from the hellebores breaking through the snow, to the magnificent sycamore which symbolizes her life.
Julia Hobart, Troy, Ohio

Past the Swimming Pool

The gravel path leads us past the gleaming woodland swimming pool, quietly shadowed by the forest background. Giant oak, hickory, and basswood trees reach skyward.

The Aullwood Sycamore

Just across Wiles Creek, the massive and imposing Aullwood sycamore looms over the woodland like a gentle giant. A nearby sign states, "This is the Aullwood sycamore, a 500-year-old remnant of Ohio's primeval forest, that was a sapling when Christopher Columbus stepped onto American shores in 1492."

The Rear Lawn

Just past the Aullwood sycamore we enter an expansive lawn at the rear of the Aull home. Scattered across the lawn are a dozen or so tall, lean sycamore trees with upper trunks and branches as white as snow. The expansive rock and fern garden, meandering garden borders, winding Wiles Creek, and dense forest make this sycamore lawn a treasured spot. The tranquil beauty here touches the emotions of all in our group today.

Rose and Lilac Gardens

We cross the gravel driveway and walk up a slight rise to the rose and lilac gardens. Someone points out how these neatly kept gardens present a more formal kind of beauty, and remarks how the gardens must represent many hours of loving care by Marie and her gardeners.

A Special Feeling

Departing the Aullwood Garden, we follow the gravel path along the Stillwater River to the parking area, still experiencing its peacefulness and simple beauty.

We are struck by the thought of how John and Marie's Aullwood has changed and developed since they first came to live here together and we ponder the impact that they and this special place have made on the world.

Aullwood twin sycamo
(in background

60

12. Like a Giant Sycamore

Many years have gone by since John brought Marie to Aullwood as a bride. Many changes have occurred to the land they called Aullwood.

Millions of lives have been directly touched as they experienced the sanctuary and farm or garden or got to know Marie and the Aullwood staff. Hundreds of interns, naturalists, gardeners, volunteers, and other staff trained at Aullwood have moved on to other positions, taking Aullwood's and Marie's message around the world.

It would be difficult to try to separate Marie's influence and leadership from that of Aullwood, so intertwined are they, or to estimate the breadth and depth of that influence on the quality of life, not only in the Miami Valley, but throughout the world.

They are like the branches of the giant sycamores on the Aullwood land, reaching up and out year after year and touching ever more lives.

Paul E. Knoop, Jr.
former director
Aullwood Audubon Center

Photograph by Ben Jakobowski

Marie and Susie, 1996

Aullwood sycamore crown, Aullwood Garden

Afterword

To me, Aullwood is a beautiful example of the celebration of life. At Aullwood, land, water, light, and air collide with literally thousands of plants and animals to form one magnificent environment. At Aullwood, the living are in harmony with the dying. From the largest trees to the tiniest insect, there is balance. New life is nourished from the old and provides, in the rawest of examples, the meaning of nature. Aullwood is a safe harbor from the stress and hardship of life. Here one can stop, even if only for a moment, and recharge the inner human spirit. Here at Aullwood, in sunshine and in gray, one can find beauty. Here at Aullwood one can always find peace. It is this peace that allows us to see that life truly does go on....

Kevin Kepeler
park manager, Aullwood Garden
Five Rivers MetroParks

For nearly thirty years I have watched an old dead log along the trail in Aullwood Garden return to the soil.... The rhythm of life continues.
Tom Hissong
education co-ordinator, Aullwood Audubon Center and Farm

I remember my brother Allan introducing me to Mrs. Aull and visiting her garden together, delighting with Mother as she identified bird calls at Aullwood, and walking with my brother Euie along the trails. These family members are gone now, but I feel their presence whenever I visit Aullwood.
Gail Horvath

The mature woods, the prairie, marsh, pond, pine forest, Mrs. Aull's garden: it could take a lifetime to truly know these diverse places and the wonders that they hold.
Brian S. Rayburn
former Aullwood intern

Fringed gentian